A ROOF OF TIGER LILIES

DONALD HALL

A Roof of
Tiger Lilies

POEMS

THE VIKING PRESS
NEW YORK

PUBLISHED IN 1964 BY THE VIKING PRESS, INC.
625 MADISON AVENUE, NEW YORK, N.Y. 10022
PUBLISHED SIMULTANEOUSLY IN CANADA BY
THE MACMILLAN COMPANY OF CANADA LIMITED
LIBRARY OF CONGRESS CATALOG CARD NUMBER:
64-20680

PRINTED IN GREAT BRITAIN

Acknowledgment is made to the following magazines in which these poems first appeared: *Audit, Chelsea, Encounter, Fresco, The Hudson Review, The Listener, London Times Literary Supplement, The Nation, National Review, The New-England Galaxy, New Statesman, The New Yorker, The Paris Review, Partisan Review, Poetry, Poetry North West, The Saturday Review, The Sixties, The Spectator, Wormwood Review.*

The author is grateful to the John Simon Guggenhein Memorial Foundation for a grant which enabled him to finish this book.

FOR LEONARD AND MARY STEVENS

CONTENTS

I

II

III

I

THE SNOW

Snow is in the oak.
Behind the thick, whitening
air which the wind drives,
the weight of the sun
presses the snow
on the pane of my window.

I remember snows and my walking
through their first fall in cities,
asleep or drunk
with the slow, desperate falling.
The snow blurs in my eyes
with other snows.

Snow is what must
come down, even if it struggles
to stay in the air with the strength
of the wind. Like an old man,
whatever I touch I turn
to the story of death.

Snow is what fills
the oak, and what covers
the grass and the bare garden.
Snow is what reverses
the sidewalk and the lawn
into the substance of whiteness.

[9]

So the watcher sleeps himself
back to the baby's eyes.
The tree, the breast, and the floor
are limbs of him, and from
his eyes he extends a skin
which grows over the world.

The baby is what must
have fallen, like snow. He resisted,
the way the old man
struggles inside the airy tent
to keep on breathing.
Birth is the fear of death.

Snow is what melts.
I cannot open the door
to the cycles of water.
The sun has withdrawn itself
and the snow keeps falling,
and something will always be falling.

THE FARM

Standing on top of the hay
in a good sweat,
I felt the wind from the lake,
dry on my back,
where the chaff
grew like the down on my face.

At night on the bare boards
of the kitchen,
we stood while the old man
in his nightshirt gummed
the stale crusts
of his bread and milk.

Up on the gray hill
behind the barn, the stones
had fallen away
where the Pennacook marked
a way to go
south from the narrow river.

By the side of the lake
my dead uncle's rowboat rots
in heavy bushes.
Slim pickerel glint
in the water. Black horned pout
doze on the bottom.

THE GRASS

When I look at the grass
out my window in rain,
I know that it happens
again. Under

new grass,
among stones and the downward
probe of trees,
everything builds

or alters itself.
I am led
through a warm descent
with my eyes covered,

to hear the words
of water. I listen, with
roots of
the moist grass.

The musk-ox smells
in his long head
my boat coming. When
I feel him there,
intent, heavy,

the oars make wings
in the white night,
and deep woods are close
on either side
where trees darken.

I rowed past towns
in their black sleep
to come here. I passed
the northern grass
and cold mountains.

The musk-ox moves
when the boat stops,
in hard thickets. Now
the wood is dark
with old pleasures.

The wings lacking a trunk
flap like a sail. Body
strains, follows and stiffens the
meeting of grand jellies.

It weighs air. In the wind,
blank at the low margin,
high cuts in solids of
wind are the stone footsteps.

Unbent, loosed in the thick
sky and the walked heaven,
look, how the body of
space is a steep dying.

It discovers by night
what the day hid from it.
Sometimes it turns itself
into an animal.
In summer it takes long walks
by itself where meadows
fold back from ditches.
Once it stood still
in a quiet row of machines.
Who knows
what it is thinking?

THE CHILD

He lives among a dog,
a tricycle, and a friend.
Nobody owns him.

He walks by himself, beside
the black pool, in the cave
where icicles of rock

rain hard water,
and the walls are rough
with the light of stone.

He hears some low talking
without words.
The hand of a wind touches him.

he walks until he is tired
or somebody calls him.
Then he leaves right away.

Later when he plays with his friend
he stops suddenly
to hear the black water.

In the middle distance
a tree stands,
above it a cloud.

The tree is a raised fist.
It moves so slowly
you cannot see it move.

The cloud changes.
It is almost nothing,
and the wind pushes it.

The tree is an engine
for becoming itself
in the dirt and the sun.

The cloud resembles
whatever we see there.
The tree is chopped down

to be changed entirely,
but if the cloud rips
it becomes other clouds.

The tree is hard to the hands.
To touch the cloud
hardens the touching.

THE SUN

He waited in the sadness of the sun's intention
with a toy in his hand. In cloudy weather or rain
or when the light turned to China he kept to himself
his own darkness. In the sun he knew he was followed.

THE MOON

A woman who lived
in a tree caught
the moon in a kettle.

The wind on the roof
of the tree thumped
while she built her fire.

She boiled it down
to a flat bean
to set on her plate.

She swallowed the moon
and the moon grew
like a child inside her.

When the wind flew away
she mounted
the steps of the air

to bear the moon
on a dark bed
in the house of the night.

She nurses him
while the wind perches
like a heavy bird

in the void branches
of a tree, beside
a cold kettle.

I stand at the rail
of a ship which is sailing
through the pale Atlantic.
I stare at the sea
like a monk.

. . .

I remember watching
from the porch of a cottage.
The loose bulk swayed.

. . .

She is the mother of calms
and the hot grasses;
the mother of cliffs
and of the grinding sand;
she is the mother of the dead
submarine, which rolls
on a beach among gulls.

. . .

The drunken waves argue
the same sentences
over and over, as if
no one will understand them.

THE KILL

Sheep move on the grass
so little one imagines
small boulders.

Then a dog hurtles
into the field, like water.

The sheep flutter.
The dog tears among them
for five minutes. Then he diminishes

like a wind or a flood
into the rubble of distance.

This one
   is a sail
   and catches
   the fist of
the wind.

This one
   is a dog
   and asleep
   on a rug
all day.

This one
   is an elm
   which makes shade
   on a lawn
and roosts

birds. This
   one is a
   piano
   factory.
This one

is a
   Frank Lloyd Wright
   desert house.
   This one is
gold bells.

If I said, "Little wives,
shut in your dark
houses, an enormous
tiger lily splits
the roof of each house

in the night, and arranges
the moon to itself,
and only withdraws
just at dawn,"
you would smile,

and think about bright
flowers, and forget
the money and the shopping,
but if I went on, "I only
see your lilies grow

in my happy sleep,
because you have made no gardens
in your blocks of houses
for flowers that come
in the dark night,"

you would suddenly
cry, or pick up a book,
or walk by yourselves
for a long time
on the white sidewalks.

II

AN AMERICAN IN AN ESSEX VILLAGE

He walks out of the village. The road
  lowers into a hollow
    which villagers call
  the Borough, though it contains
only a farm, a stream where small boys
      go newting,

and four mediaeval town houses
  which drop plaster in the frosts
    of winter, and which
  a decade will dismantle.
Their second storeys jut like the brows
      of children.

The road climbs, and he looks back across
  the Borough at the long Church
    like a cathedral
  with its weathered carved stone
over the planes of the red-tiled roofs.
      Dominant,

the spire pierces seven times the height
  of the beech tree. The village
    gathered by the spire
  pointed toward a destiny
which ordained the narrow proportions
      which please him.

Yet inside the Church, he remembers,
　the death-watch beetle hollows
　　six-hundred-year-old
　beams. The Vicar reconstructs
old music and Sarum liturgy
　　　for twelve souls.

He wanders South of the Church, and sees
　the derelict mill which heaves
　　among the barley
　of a high field and raises
nude vanes which the industrious wind
　　　　cannot turn.

He walks toward it, on lanes through barley.
　Its pitted red brick is dark
　　against the green hills
　opening past the village.
In a century of poor gleanings
　　　it crushed wheat

for everyone's dark loaf. Its wide cone
　taught the proportions of use.
　　Its ruin appals
　only an eye which invents
a landscape which needs it. It is there
　　　to be climbed.

In the complicated village street
　to which he descends, a truck

delivers milled flour
to the baker in his shop.
The curved street is a continuous
delicate

pargetting, and beyond the resumed
almoners' house, gas pumps lean
from the imagined
plaster and timber. He hears
the Vicar teaching his old cello
to the son

of the Tory grocer in the room
at the back of the grocer's
under the low oak
beams with the ship's markings on them,
which ten years of winter without heat
would crumble.

He goes home and makes tea at a stove
in a house which will vanish.
If he spills water
from kettle onto cokestove
it hurtles together from all sides
at once.

A Roman road took us from the village of Bradwell-
    on-Sea through marshy crop farms down to the shore
      on a ridge which was so gradual

my friend had to point it out. Yet in a tidal flood
    the road is a strip of dry land in a plain
      of water. Now the sloping meadows

erupted with the lean daffodils of March. We walked
    tilting our bodies against the Northern wind.
      In the ditches there were crumbling rows

of four-foot concrete trylons. "One Sunday in nineteen-
    forty, we set branches in the largest fields
      to stop the gliders." A radar screen

turned in its arc to the north, looking out to the sea,
    and gulls swooped at the Nuclear Power Station
      as if it were a ship. Beyond it

the estuary washed inland as far as Maldon,
    and tied near the banks were the left-over bodies
      of freighters and tankers hung on chains,

the trash of a long war, and of an economy
    of sailors. Ahead of us, where the road struck
      straight at the sea, the afternoon sun

illuminated a narrow stone barn. "St. Peter's,"
    said my friend, "where Bishop Cedd made his mission
        to Saxons in six-hundred-fifty."

It backed up close to the cold sea that expected it,
    like the last king of a defeated nation
        beaten from its plains by invaders.

The sun made black shadows within the stone and tile wall,
    as rough as if the sea wind had worked at it
        to raise the surfaces like landscape.

"The new brick of the side is where farmers hacked a door
    to turn it into a barn. It was only
        eighty-odd years ago that someone

"saw that it was Cedd's St. Peter's, and changed it again
    back to a church." The Bishop had scavenged tiles
        from the Roman fort of Othona

which had held the mouth of the estuary against
    Saxon pillagers, until the Romans left
        to defend their own city. Inside,

rubble was heaped in the corners. It was a bare room
    without grace or comfort. More bricks had filled in
        Cedd's narrow arches, but the color

of the new brick revealed the old shapes. We went outside
    and found a piece of the thick wall which remains
        of Othona. "Out there in the marsh,"

[28]

my friend told me, "when they made tank trenches they dug up
     cartloads of Roman sea-wall. We were waiting
          for a new invasion from the sea."

We walked for a moment under the noise of the gulls,
     and then returned to the village, on the road
          which keeps its head out of the water.

for George Scrivener

Your letter describes
    what you see from your window. You chose,
among the council
    houses and gray cities, to observe

a destroyed abbey
    whose stones you touch for their proportion,
the lines of a mind
    although the mind is dead. I write you

from an old attic
    where the green of maples like a storm
cuts off my winter
    prospect of square blocks of the same house.

Maples are the past,
    for the settlers liked a good shade tree.
On the older blocks,
    ugly frame houses like ours recall

the German merchants
    who left their country to avoid war.
Rural Michigan
    took them in. It is sentimental

to love their houses
    for being burly like them, and trees
too are evasions.
    In America, the past exists

in the library.
      It is not the wind on the old stone.
The wind blows in you
      like power, and the blades of the mill turn.

Unmeasured voices
      shed lies in their vying to utter
like leaves from maples.
      Yet the loose roads and the twelve seasons

allow us to move.
      It is what we like most in ourselves.
Most of your country
      envies our worst houses, and would sell

abbeys if they could
      to Americans who collect. Some
here try to construct
      a new abbey without architects

or an idea,
      except to represent the shapeless
shape of a nation.
      All of them scatter with the dry leaves.

But the best of us
      have resembled instead the raiding
millionaires; without
      history, we pillage history,

and return loaded
        with castles and pagodas, temples
to various gods
        whom we invoke in borrowed costume,

fifteen languages
        half-learned but poems well-translated,
and a collection
        of whatever happened everywhere.

Perhaps this warehouse
        of stones is apter at deception
than native ruins,
        but who lacks parents adopts the world.

"What is it you're mumbling, old Father, my Dad?
Come drink up your soup and I'll put you to bed."

"By the Exeter River, by the river, I said."

"Stop dreaming of rivers, old Father, my Dad,
Or save all your dreaming till you're tucked in bed."

"It was cold by the river. We came in a sled."

"It's colder to think of, old Father, my Dad,
Than the blankets and bolsters and pillows of bed."

"We took off his dress and the cap from his head."

"Undressed in the winter, old Father, my Dad?
What could you be thinking? Let's get off to bed."

"And Sally, poor Sally I reckon is dead."

"Was she an old sweetheart, old Father, my Dad?
Now lean on my shoulder and come up to bed."

"We drowned your half-brother. I remember we did."

Often I saw, as on my balcony
   I stirred the afternoon into my tea,
Enamelled swards descending to the *Thames*,
   Called *Isis* here, and flowers that were gems,
Cattle in herds, and great senescent trees,
   Through which, as Pope predicted, ran the breeze.
Ad sinistram, where limpid *Cherwell* flows,
   Often I saw the punts of gallant beaux
Who sang like shepherds to each gentle love
   Quaint tales of Trojan warriors to prove
That loving Maidens are rewarded here
   With bastards and with pints of watered beer.
Here too I saw my countrymen at large,
   Expending *Kodachrome* upon a barge.
From chauffered *Car*, or touring *Omnibus*,
   They leered at me, calling me 'them', not 'us'.
A jutting woman came to me and said,
   "Your *Highness*, can those big white geese be fed?"
"*Yankee* go home," I snarled. "Of course the *Swans*,
   As the *Bard* puts it, are reserved for *Dons*."
She fainted then, beside two *Christ Church* porters,
   Who cast her, as I told them, on the waters.

III

Ten years ago this minute, he possibly sat
in the sunlight, in Connecticut, in an old chair:
a car may have stopped in the street outside;
he may have turned his head; his ear may have itched.
Since it was September, he probably saw
single leaves dropping from the maple tree.
If he was reading, he turned back to his book,
and perhaps the smell of roses in a pot
came together with the smell of cheese sandwiches
and the smell of a cigarette
smoked by his brother who was not dead then.

The moments of that day dwindled
to the small notations of clocks,
and the day busily became another day,
and another, and today, when his hand moves
from his ear which still itches
to rest on his leg, it is marked with the passage
of ten years. Suddenly he has the idea
that thousands and thousands of his days
lie stacked into the ground
like leaves, or like that pressure of green
which turns into coal in a million years.

Though leaves rot, or leaves burn in the gutter;
though the complications of this morning's breakfast
dissolve in faint shudders of light

at a great distance, he continues to daydream
that the past is a country under the ground
where the days practise their old habits
over and over, as faint and persistent
as cigarette smoke in an airless room.
He wishes he could travel there like a tourist
and photograph the unseizable days
in the sunlight, in Connecticut, in an old chair.

In the kitchen of the old house, late,
I was making some coffee
   and I day-dreamed sleepily of old friends.
Then the dream turned. I waited.
   I walked alone all day in the town
where I was born. It was cold,
   a Saturday in January
when nothing happens. The streets
   changed as the sky grew dark around me.
The lamps in the small houses
   had tassels on them, and the black cars
at the curb were old and square.
   A ragman passed with his horse, their breaths
blooming like white peonies,
   when I turned into a darker street
and I recognized the house
   from snapshots. I felt as separate
as if the city and the house
   were closed inside a globe which I shook
to make it snow. No sooner
   did I think of snow, but snow started
to fill the heavy darkness
   around me. It reflected the glare
of the streetlight as it fell
   melting on the warmth of the sidewalk
and frozen on frozen grass.
   Then I heard out of the dark the sound
of steps on the bare cement
   in a familiar rhythm. Under

[37]

the streetlight, bent to the snow,
     hatless, younger than I, so young that
I was not born, my father
     walked home to his bride and his supper.
A shout gathered inside me
     like a cold wind, to break the rhythm,
to keep him from entering
     that heavy door – but I stood under
a tree, closed in by the snow,
     and did not shout, to tell what happened
in twenty years, in winter,
     when his early death grew inside him
like snow piling on the grass.
     He opened the door and met the young
woman who waited for him.

John Fleming walked in the house his cousin left him
and wanted the very tick of the old stopped clock.
He wanted nothing of his own past. He wanted
the hour of the day at which an heiress was born
or the portrait finished of a virtuous Aunt;
the temperature and the weather, the exact
feel of it, the sound and the stillness from the street
and the park, and the slant on the walls of the light
of afternoons that had been. He learned to enter
the intimate centuries of walnut sideboards,
to drowse with mahogany chairs, and to endure
with old tables the spill of good wine. He listened
when the stilled voices of the scrutable past
spoke, faintly and fine, from a mirror where he saw
no shadow of himself – the glass mottled with age –
but the resemblance of invisible girls,
Victorian ringlets and Alexandra fringe,
primping before a man they would not have cared for,
the beau of the dead, the gallant of dead ladies.

partly quoted from Henry James' The Sense of the Past

The horses of the sea; remember
how the sea paws at its moving floor,
charging and failing. The mane on his
neck arched exactly in strength matches
the tail at the bend of waves breaking
on opposite shores. He is the king
of the wild waves, charging and failing.
When Master Zeus struck from the North, he
drove Poseidon the Horse to the sea.
Sacred to Poseidon are both the
nimble dolphin and the stiff pine tree.

for Robert and Carol Bly

PLACES

1. New Hampshire

A bear sleeps in a cellar hole; pine needles
heap over a granite doorstep; a well brims
with acorns and the broken leaves of an oak
which grew where an anvil rested in a forge.

My eyes close; I can see another summer:
a bark of rust grows on the tree of a gas pump,
EAT signs gather like leaves in the shallow
cellars of diners; a wildcat waits for deer

on the roof of a car. Blacktop buckled by frost
starts goldenrod from the highway. Fat honey bees
meander among raspberries, where a quarrel
of vines crawls into the spilled body of a plane.

2. Southwest of Buffalo

The long lakes, flanked
by the conservative
farms, which are asleep
but thinking, collect
water from the quiet
hills, which as they slope
and touch, make towns
to hide from the wind.
Near Ellington, in the Randolph

graveyard, Albert Gallatin Dow,
who died a hundred years old
in nineteen-eight,
remains in the granite tomb
which he ordered built
towards the day when the short beard
of even a centenarian
would blow in the wind
of flowers, on
the hills of New York.

3. Mycenae

In the shaft graves, butterflies
of gold flutter at the gold
masks of the Cretan traders.

Over the gate, the simple
lions of the Achaeans
stand upright in old combat.

The King climbed the long carpet
to be struck like a zebra
drinking at a water-hole.

4. The City of Grandfathers

The rows of workers' houses in Millvillage
wove carpets in Turkey

to deepen floors in the house
which slept
on the river, out of sight of blocks
of black brick houses
on the far side of the two-sided hill.
The delicate
sister among the willows
carried herself as if she were old China.

In the closet of her father's trees, she hummed
a French song to the flowers
which did not smell of the smoke
which lay
in the streets of Millvillage, and sat
with her new sketch book
spread on her lap, thinking of younger sons
from Burke's, and caught
in her new Japanese lines
the twisted run of the polluted river.

The learned King fought
like a fool, flanked
and outtricked, who hacked
in a corner of cousins
until the ten thousand
swords lay broken,
and the women walked
in their houses alone.

On a journey among horses,
the spirit of a man who died
only a week ago
is walking through heather
and forgets that its body
had seventy years.
Wild horses are singing,
and voices of the rocks.

The spirit from the bone-yard
finds a new life, in the field
where the King's wound
built the blackness of Glasgow
and the smoke of the air.
The spirit, like a boy,
picks up from the heather
a whole sword.

in memory of Edwin Muir

What the birds say
is colored. Shade
feels the thickness
shrubs make in a
July growth,

heavy brown thorns
for Autumn, curled
horns in double
rows. Listening
the birds fly

down, in shade. Leaves
of darkness turn
inward, noises
curve inward, and
the seed talks.

from a sculpture of Henry Moore

As they grew older,
the land which had grown wheat
washed down the hill,
and the river
carried the land into the sea.

The priest with the horned
mask, who brought meat
from the altar,
turned into a bird
and flew among mountains.

The people of the markets
who touched their heads to the ground,
changed into clumps of weed
among the gutters
of the bare hill.

The King and Queen rule
over the dark nation
of thrones. As slowly
as a river builds a delta,
they have become still.

from Henry Moore's sculpture

[46]

"RECLINING FIGURE"

Then the knee of the wave
turned to stone.

By the cliff of her flank
I anchored,

in the darkness of harbors
laid-by.

from Henry Moore's sculptures

When he lies in the night away from her,
the backs of his eyelids burn.
He turns in the darkness as if it were an oven.
The flesh parches and he lies awake
thinking of everything wrong.

He remembers the name of a man
and a weekend before they loved each other.
His mind in its tight corner
watches a scene by the ocean last summer.
Or is it next summer he watches?

In the morning when he goes to meet her,
his heart struggles at his ribs
like an animal trapped in its burrow.
Then he sees her running to meet him,
red faced with hurry and cold.

She stumbles over the snow.
Her knees above orange knee-socks
bob in a froth of the hems
of skirt and coat and petticoat.
Her eyes have not shut all night.

As I watched, the animals
that lived in her shoulders
broke from their cages.

They prowled the room
with its ivory carvings.
They were lions!

They roared, and I thought
that I would be eaten
Well, I was ready,

but she shrugged her shoulders
and the wild lions
returned to their cages.

This heroine, this thicket
of lions smiled
between ivory earrings.

D

Here is a fat animal, a bear
that is partly a dodo.
Ridiculous wings hang at his shoulders
as if they were collarbones
while he plods in the bad brickyards
at the edge of the city smiling
and eating flowers. He eats them
because he loves them
because they are beautiful
because they love him.
It is eating flowers which makes him fat.
He carries his huge stomach
over the gutters of damp leaves
in the parking lots in October,
but inside that paunch
he knows there are fields of lupine
and meadows of mustard and poppy.
He encloses sunshine.
Winds bend the flowers
in combers across the valley,
birds hang on the stiff wind,
at night there are showers, and the sun
lifts through a haze every morning
of the summer in the stomach.

AN AIRSTRIP IN ESSEX, 1960

It is a lost road into the air.
It is a desert
among sugar beets.
The tiny wings
of the Spitfires of nineteen-forty-one
flake in the mud of the Channel.

Near the road a brick pillbox
totters under a load of grass,
where Home Guards waited
in the white fogs of the invasion winter.

Goodnight, old ruined war.

In Poland the wind rides on a jagged wall.
Smoke rises from the stones; no, it is mist.

the spider glints
he is huge he is made of aluminum
slowly the crane lowers him
outside a glass building
his legs crawl in the air
he dangles turning
by a steel thread
the sun splits on his metal skin
no one sees him

I kneel at a wooden box
in shade in silence
eye-socket touches felt eyepiece
a car rolls slowly
into the crossed hairs
a head
enters the segments of a circle
hairs cross on a head
I squeeze slowly

the crane lifts the spider slowly
his legs retracting
he becomes a sphere a point
glinting aluminum
no one sees him
the crane swerves him over a ledge
his nest on a high building
humming in a cement hole
electric glass

IV

I lived in a dry well
under the rank grass of a meadow.

A white ladder leaned out of it
but I was afraid of the sounds

of animals grazing.
I crouched by the wall ten years

until the circle of a woman's darkness
moved over mine like a mouth.

The ladder broke out in leaves
and fruit hung from the branches.

I climbed to the meadow grass.
I drink from the well of cattle.

The avenue rises toward a city of white marble.
I am not meeting anyone. The capitol is empty.
I enter the dome of sleep.

. . .

I was lying on the sofa to rest, to sleep
a few minutes, perhaps.
I felt my body sag into the hole of sleep.
All at once I was awake and frightened.
My own death was drifting near me
in the middle of life. The strong body
blurred and diminished into the dark waters.
The flesh floated away.

. . .

The shadow is a tight passage
that no one will be spared
who goes down
to the deep well.
In sleep, something remembers.
Three times since I woke
from the first sleep,
it has drunk that water.
Awake, it is still sleeping.

1

Today they cut down the oak.
Strong men climbed with ropes
in the brittle tree.
The exhaust of a gasoline saw
was blue in the branches.

It is February. The oak has been dead a year.
I remember the great sails of its branches
rolling out greenly, a hundred and twenty feet up,
and acorns thick on the lawn.
Nine cities of squirrels lived in that tree.
Today they ran over the snow
squeaking their lamentation.

Yet I was happy that it was coming down.
"Let it come down!" I kept saying to myself
with a joy that was strange to me.
Though the oak was the shade of old summers,
I loved the guttural saw.

2

By night a nude trunk stands up fifteen feet,
and cords of firewood press
on the twiggy frozen grass of the yard.
A man comes every afternoon for a week
to cut the trunk down to the grass.

[55]

Bluish stains spread through the wood
and make it harder to cut.
He says they are the nails of a trapper
who dried his pelts on the oak
when badgers dug in my lawn.

At the bottom he hacks for two days,
his knuckles scraping the stiff snow.
His chain saw breaks three teeth.
He cannot make the trunk smooth. He leaves
one night after dark.

3

Roots stiffen under the ground
and the frozen street, coiled around pipes and wires.
The stump is a platform of blond wood
in the gray winter. It is nearly level
with the snow that covers the little garden around it.
It is a door into the underground of old summers,
but if I bend down to it, I am lost
in crags and buttes of a harsh landscape
that goes on forever. When snow melts
the wood darkens into the ground;
rain and thawed snow move deeply into the stump,
backwards along the disused tunnels.

4

The edges of the trunk turn black.
In the middle there is a pale overlay,
like a wash of chalk on darkness.

The desert of the winter
has moved inside.
I do not step on it now, I am used to it,
like a rock, or a bush that does not grow.

There is a sailing ship
beached in the cove of a small island
where the warm water is turquoise.
The hulk leans over, full of rain and sand,
and shore flowers grow from it.
Then it is under full sail in the Atlantic,
on a blue day, heading for the island.

She has planted sweet alyssum
in the holes where the wood was rotten.
It grows thick, it bulges
like flowers contending from a tight vase.
Now the stump sinks downward into its roots
with a cargo of rain
and white blossoms that last into October.

He discovers himself on an old airfield.
He thinks he was there before,
but rain has washed out the lettering of a sign.
A single biplane, all struts and wires,
stands in the long grass and wildflowers.
He pulls himself into the narrow cockpit
although his muscles are stiff
and sits like an egg in a nest of canvas.
He sees that the machine gun has rusted.
The glass over the instruments
has broken, and the red arrows are gone
from his gas gauge and his altimeter.
When he looks up, his propeller is turning,
although no one was there to snap it.
He lets out the throttle. The engine catches
and the propeller spins into the wind.
He bumps over holes in the grass,
and he remembers to pull back on the stick.
He rises from the land in a high bounce
which gets higher, and suddenly he is flying again.
He feels the old fear, and rising over the fields
the old gratitude. In the distance, circling
in a beam of late sun like birds migrating,
there are the wings of a thousand biplanes.
He banks and flies to join them.

in memory of Philip Thompson, d. 1960

One midnight, after a day when lilies
lift themselves out of the ground while you watch them,
and you come into the house at dark
your fingers grubby with digging, your eyes
vague with the pleasure of digging,

let a wind raised from the South
climb through your bedroom window, lift you in its arms
– you have become as small as a seed –
and carry you out of the house, over the black garden,
spinning and fluttering,

and drop you in cracked ground.
The dirt will be cool, rough to your clasped skin
like a man you have never known.
You will die into the ground
in a dead sleep, surrendered to water.

You will wake suffering
a widening pain in your side, a breach
gapped in your tight ribs
where a green shoot struggles to lift itself upwards
through the tomb of your dead flesh

to the sun, to the air of your garden
where you will blossom
in the shape of your own self, thoughtless
with flowers, speaking
to bees, in the language of green and yellow, white and red.

At the edge of the city the pickerel
who has lost his way
vomits and dies. The river
with its white hair staggers to the sea.

My life lay open like a smashed car.

Windows barred, ivy, square stone.
Lines gather at her mouth and her eyes
like cracks in a membrane.
While I watch, eyeballs and tongue
spill on the tiled floor
in a puddle of yolks and whites.

The intact 707
under the clear wave, the sun shining.

The playhouse of my grandfather's mother
stands north of the shed; spiders
and the dolls' teacups of dead women.
In Ohio the K-Mart shrugs;
it knows it is going to die.

A stone, the closed eye of the dirt.

I walked outside before dawn
past closed houses thick with breath.
A door clicked; a light opened.
Houses sailed up
like wrecks from the bottom of the sea.

But if the world is a dream
the puffed stomach of Juan is a dream
and the rich in Connecticut are dreaming.

There are poor bachelors
who live in shacks made of oilcans
and broken doors, who stitch their shirts
until the cloth disappears under stitches,
who collect nails in tin cans.

The wind is exhausted.

In the middle of the road of my life
I wake walking in a field.
A trolley car comes out of the elms,
the tracks laid through an acre of wheat stubble,
slanting downhill. I board it,
and cross the field into the new pine.

COLD WATER

I step around a gate of bushes
in the mess
and trickle of a dammed stream
and my shoe fills with cold water. I
enter the shade
of a thicket, a black pool,
a small circle of stunned drowsing air,

vaulted with birch which meets overhead
as if smoke
rose up and turned into leaves.
I stand on the roots of a maple
and imagine
dropping a line. My wrist jumps
with the pain of a live mouth hooked deep,

and I stare, and watch where the lithe stripe
tears water.
Then it heaves on my hand: cold,
squaretailed, flecked, revenant flesh
of a Brook Trout.
The pine forests I walked through
darken and cool a dead farmer's brook.

I look up and see the Iroquois
coming back
standing among the birches
on the other side of the black pool.

[62]

The five elders
have come for me, I am young,
my naked body whitens with cold

in the snow, blisters in the bare sun,
the ice cuts
me, the thorns of blackberries:
I am ready for the mystery.
I follow them
over the speechless needles
of pines which are dead or born again.